SHAWN MENDES

It's My Time

by Debra Mostow Zakarin

Scholastic Inc.

UNAUTHORIZED:
This book is not sponsored by or affiliated with Shawn Mendes or anyone involved with him.

TABLE OF CONTENTS

Chapter 1:
SIX SECONDS TO FAME

I magine going to bed one night and waking up the next morning as one of the most popular singers on the Internet. Impossible? Shawn Mendes would have thought so, too, except it happened to him!

One night, Shawn's younger sister, Aaliyah, asked him to record a cover of Justin Bieber's song "As Long as You Love Me." Shawn recorded a six-second clip of himself playing guitar and singing an acoustic version of the song. He thought it was good—not great—although he had been practicing a lot. Shawn uploaded it onto the video app Vine and went to sleep. The next morning he had 10,000 likes. Just a couple of months later, Shawn had over 200,000 followers!

Shawn knew he was on to something big, and he was right. Just one month after uploading that very first Vine, he performed his debut concert in Toronto, Canada. And that was just the beginning of Shawn's rise to stardom.

Chapter 2:
HOME BASE

Shawn Peter Raul Mendes was born on August 8, 1998, in Toronto, Ontario, Canada. He was raised in a suburb called Pickering where he still lives with his parents and sister, Aaliyah, who is five years younger. His mom, Karen, is a real estate agent, and his dad, Manuel, is a businessman.

Shawn and Aaliyah are close and like to spend time together. They even post covers together sometimes. It's absolutely the cutest thing to watch them sing together!

Music was always playing in Shawn's house. His parents listened to reggae, rock, and country music. Shawn isn't quite sure where his musical talent comes from since neither of his parents sing or play instruments. But his parents are

involved in everything he does. Shawn was in the car with his mom the day he heard that record labels were interested in meeting him. She received an email from his manager and they were both freaking out together. "It was really funny," Shawn told *Digital Spy*.

Now when Shawn drives around his home city of Toronto, he can't believe it when one of his songs comes on the radio. Smiling to himself, he looks at the other cars on the highway and wonders who else is listening, too. It's hard for Shawn to describe the feeling. "It's good. It's super weird, but it's good," Shawn told 97.1 AMP Radio.

So much of Shawn's life has changed. But it is his family who really helps him to remember who he is, and what's important. Shawn told *Digital Spy*, "There are times when I'm super overwhelmed . . . but I think what's keeping me calm, and who I am by staying true to

myself, is my whole family being so supportive and keeping me grounded." He added, "They treat me the exact same way they treated me years and years ago."

Chapter 3:
SELF-MADE MUSICIAN

It wasn't too long ago that Shawn was just like any other high school student. He liked to hang out with his friends. They would go longboarding and play hockey and soccer. He was in the glee club, and he even played Prince Charming when he took acting lessons. But the one experience at school that really left its mark on Shawn was being part of Leadership Camp. That's where he learned self-confidence and leadership skills. In an interview for his school, Shawn said he doesn't think he would have been able to achieve some of his goals without his experience there. It was so important, Shawn wanted all students to be able to take part in the camp—whether they had the money or not. So, in order to give back

to his school, Shawn organized a benefit concert to raise money for kids who couldn't afford to go. And of course, Shawn performed.

Shawn first started singing in elementary school, and even back then his classmates told him how great he sounded. This motivated Shawn, and he set a goal to get better each day. Believe it or not, Shawn learned to sing more from watching YouTube cover songs than from listening to the original versions.

At first, Shawn hated how he sounded, but his followers were always very encouraging. "If you look at YouTube and see some of my first covers you will hear that I don't sound good. But I . . . wanted so much to be good at it that I forced myself to figure out what sounds right and what sounds wrong," Shawn told *The Telegraph*. "I'm not the best singer in the world; I'm just good at picking up what I want to sound like."

A few years before his big break, Shawn taught himself how to play guitar by watching YouTube videos and practicing a lot. The very first song he learned how to play on the guitar was "Hey, Soul Sister" by Train. Shawn explained to *The Telegraph*, "I taught myself these chords I didn't know the name of and slowly started to get the hang. I was obsessed with it. Every day I'd play and think, *I'm not good enough yet; I need to get better*. Then I'd play for hours and hours."

Chapter 4:
A POP STAR UPLOADED

In August 2013, Shawn uploaded that now famous six-second video. "I was just doing it for fun," Shawn told *The Telegraph*. "But then I realized that actually no one else was using Vine like that, so I thought, *I'm going to take advantage of this and try to make something of it*." Vine was an amazing creative outlet for Shawn. His fans really loved that he wasn't trying to just "copy" how the artists sang, but he put his own twist on each song.

Shawn continued to post covers for lots of awesome songs like "Give Me Love" by Ed Sheeran, "She Looks So Perfect" by 5 Seconds of Summer, and "Wanted" by Hunter Hayes. He also began posting his own original songs. His videos spread across Vine, YouTube,

Instagram, and Twitter. Suddenly, Shawn had millions of views. *Billboard* dubbed him, "Music's first Vine star."

Shawn kept gaining more followers, and they are all very important to him. Shawn would ask for their feedback and what they wanted him to sing. He really cares about their opinions. "We work as a team," Shawn said. "When I grow, they grow."

A month after posting that first video, Shawn performed in front of an audience of 600 in Toronto. "I'd been playing guitar less than a year and wasn't very good at it so it was super nerve-racking," Shawn admitted to *The Telegraph.* Shawn performed eight songs, and his fans thought he was awesome. And they were excited that his songs lasted more than six seconds.

After his first concert, there was no stopping Shawn. He toured as a member of the MAGCON Tour with other social media stars like Jack & Jack, Nash Grier, Cameron Dallas, Matthew Espinosa, and Aaron Carpenter. He also went on tour as the opening act for Austin Mahone and Fifth Harmony—so cool!

Shawn didn't need much when he was the opening act—just a stool and his guitar. He liked being able to showcase his voice and just sing. Shawn was a natural performer, and he would chat with the audience between sets. And when he'd flash his sweet smile, the fans would go wild.

Chapter 5:
LIFE OF THE PARTY

In March 2014, Shawn won the "Best Cover Song" contest on RyanSeacrest.com with his cover of "Say Something" by A Great Big World. Wearing his trademark T-shirt and hoodie, Shawn put his own spin on the song as he played the guitar and soulfully sang his heart out, beating 30 other contestants.

Shawn's manager, Andrew Gertler, discovered him when he was checking out people online who had covered "Say Something." Andrew was blown away by Shawn and instantly recognized his star quality. He contacted Shawn's mom and soon he was signed to Island Records. Shawn released his first single, "Life of the Party," in June 2014. Fans really liked the message in his song about being ordinary and making mistakes.

Someone just like them was able to understand just how hard it can be to fit in. "The meaning behind 'Life of the Party' is to be yourself and love who you are as an individual. Be confident!" Shawn told *Teen.com*.

Being himself definitely paid off because "Life of the Party" was a huge success. It was released at 11:15 p.m. and was number one by midnight. The song made Shawn the youngest artist to debut a song in the top 25 on the *Billboard* Hot 100. Shawn's EP reached number one on iTunes in just 37 minutes, and it was in the top 10 in 33 countries. "What really freaked me out," Shawn told *Digital Spy*, "was in the UK, when I went to bed it was at number 68, and then when I woke up in the morning it was at eight. I was blown away."

That same year, Shawn won a Teen Choice Award in the music category for Most Popular Web Star. And *Time* magazine included him in

its list of the 25 most influential teens of 2014. Shawn was on a roll. But even with all the success, Shawn works hard to keep it real. "I can see why people change," he explained to *Teen Vogue*. "You get complimented all the time, driven around in [a] black SUV—your life is crazy. But that's your career, not you."

Chapter 6:
INSPIRATION

Shawn's main influences are John Mayer and Ed Sheeran. "I definitely look up to those two guys a lot," Shawn told *Teen Vogue*. "Ed Sheeran is my biggest influence. I feel like as I watch him perform I'm learning." Shawn added, "The way he performs is just incredible and I'd say my style has a bit of Ed Sheeran in it."

And now, Ed Sheeran is a friend of Shawn's—how cool! Not only do they get together, but Shawn texts him whenever he feels like it. When they first met, Ed gave Shawn some great advice. He said to go to every interview and radio station. Shawn agrees with Ed that putting yourself out there helps to get you further.

Shawn is completely involved with writing the songs for his albums and it's one of his favorite parts. "I don't think it's worth doing something like this if I'm not 100 percent into it—every single song that comes out, every single picture, I want to know what it looks like and what it sounds like," he told *Just Jared Jr.* "I want to know all that stuff because if it doesn't come out being shown how I want it to be shown, then it's wrong. With the music, that is the most important part."

Most of Shawn's songs are not based on his personal life. Many of them are just stories that he has made up to try to create an emotion. And he's still learning about writing. "Every time I write a song my approach changes. I feel like every time I write a song it feels like the first time," Shawn told *Digital Spy.* "It's just as hard, it doesn't get easier but that's why I love it: because it's a challenge every time."

Shawn also feels like the challenge helps him improve as a songwriter. In the same interview he said, "I also feel like I'm learning new ways. Personally I think some songs are better than others but there was definitely progression throughout the whole writing progress."

Cameron Dallas and Shawn

Chapter 7:
SHAWNEES

S hawn loves performing in different cities, and everywhere he goes he is greeted by screaming fans. His fans are known as "Mendes Army" or "Shawnees." Shawn is blown away by the attention. But when he was making his music, Shawn never really thought about fame and attention. "I don't know what I was expecting," Shawn told *Teen Vogue*. "I kind of came in blind and it's really been incredible."

Shawn's fans are very loyal and he appreciates all of them. He takes the time to meet hundreds of them before his concerts and poses for lots of selfies. He never forgets that his fans are more than a crowd—they are real people.

Shawn interacts with his fans online, too. He has four million followers on Vine and more than three million followers each on Twitter and Instagram. When Shawn's fans tweeted about the premiere of the "Life of the Party" video over two million times, he thanked them by moving up the release of his full-length debut album, *Handwritten*!

Chapter 8:
CHILLING OUT

Before a concert, it's important for Shawn to chill out. He tries to forget just how many people he will be performing in front of. Even superstars can get nervous! He also runs through his songs and gets his voice ready. Shawn's friends keep him grounded, too. They treat him just like they did before he became a pop star—although sometimes they tease him about being a celeb. But Shawn just laughs with them. They like to hang out, play Xbox, and eat. And, while Shawn doesn't have a girlfriend right now, he really likes girls who are funny and like to dance.

Shawn is super into fitness and loves working out. That means lots of trips to the gym. Shawn posted before-and-after pictures on Instagram

Shawn and Meghan Trainor

and it's obvious his hard work is paying off. "Working out has changed my life for the best. It not only keeps me healthy and strong, but it keeps me mentally straight," Shawn explained to *Twist* magazine.

Shawn tries to take care of himself by eating right, too. His go-to healthy meal is chicken and rice, and some vegetables. But Shawn also likes to have his favorite cereals while on tour—and he can usually eat three bowls at a time!

Chapter 9:
LOOKING AHEAD

Shawn Mendes has come a long way since that night he uploaded a cover video before bed. Now he's a world-famous pop star! His full-length debut album *Handwritten* was released in April 2015 and it hit number one on the Billboard 200 chart. Shawn is feeling good about his music. "It's really unique. There's some stuff you might not have been expecting," he told *Sugarscape*. "It's very me and I'm excited about it." And while it's hard for him to pick which song from the album he likes best, he does consider "A Little Too Much" and "Never Be Alone" as two of his favorites.

Shawn also started touring in 2015. He was the opening act for Taylor Swift's The 1989 World Tour in May 2015. But first, he began

his own world tour in February 2015. Shawn still can't believe it. "It's like, wow, I sold out this place. It's more pressure. It's more exciting. It's everything," he told *Teen Vogue*. "You just feel like you're growing as an artist. It just feels really cool, like, this is your show. It says 'Shawn Mendes' not 'opening act Shawn Mendes.'"

Shawn loves life on the road. But he does admit that if he could have one superpower he would want the ability to teleport. And just where would he want to go? "I would just teleport everywhere and be in my bed every single night," Shawn told 97.1 AMP Radio.

Shawn still can't believe that he is a pop star. It's like a dream that's never ending—and his fans hope it doesn't end anytime soon.

QUICK FACTS

BIRTHDAY: August 8, 1998

ZODIAC SIGN: Leo

HEIGHT: 6' 2"

FAVE EMOJI: smirk

BIGGEST FEAR: being in the ocean by himself

FAVORITE SUBJECT IN SCHOOL: music

FAVORITE CAR: Jeep

FAVORITE FOOD: muffins

MOST-HATED FOOD: tomatoes

FAVE CHILDHOOD POSSESSION: stuffed lion named Leo

CELEBRITY CRUSH: Rachel McAdams

FAVE POSTED VINE: "Summertime Sadness"

DREAM DUET PARTNER: Eminem

MOST SURREAL MOMENT: being on the *Ellen* show

OFFICIAL TWITTER: @ShawnMendes

OFFICIAL INSTAGRAM: @shawnmendes

OFFICIAL VINE: Shawn Mendes